بِسْمِ اللهِ الرَّحْمٰنِ الرَّحِيمِ

Jewels of the Ahl al-Bayt

63 Hadith narrated by or concerning the
beloved Family of the Messenger of Allah

Compiled by
Luqman al-Andalusi

Title: Jewels of the Ahl al-Bayt
Author: Luqman al-Andalusi
Islamic Calligraphy: Courtesy of the Prince Ghazi Trust

First Edition

ISBN-13: 978-0-9984380-2-3
ISBN-10: 0-9984380-2-2

Questions pertaining to Jawahir Media may be directed to
jewelsandalusi@gmail.com.

بسم الله الرحمن الرحيم

Jawahir Media is dedicated to the propagation of books concerning the Ahl al-Kisa (The People of the Cloak).

Peace be upon them all.

Thank you for your support Hermano.
May الله bless you with every good ان شاء الله

Contents

Jewels of the Ahl al-Bayt

Hadith 1

حَدَّثَنَا عُثْمَانُ بْنُ أَبِي شَيْبَةَ، حَدَّثَنَا عَبْدَةُ، عَنْ هِشَامِ بْنِ عُرْوَةَ، عَنْ أَبِيهِ، عَنْ عَائِشَةَ، قَالَتْ بَشَّرَ رَسُولُ اللَّهِ صَلَّى اللَّهُ عَلَيْهِ وَسَلَّمَ خَدِيجَةَ بِنْتَ خُوَيْلِدٍ بِبَيْتٍ فِي الْجَنَّةِ .

(The mother of the believers) - Aisha (bint Abi Bakr al-Siddique), Allah be pleased with them, reported that the Messenger of Allah ﷺ gave glad tidings to (his first and most beloved wife) Khadijah bint Khuwaylid, Allah be pleased with her, of a palace in Paradise.[1]

---

1 Sahih Muslim – Sahih Hadith

Hadith 2

حَدَّثَنِي أَحْمَدُ بْنُ أَبِي رَجَاءٍ، حَدَّثَنَا النَّضْرُ، عَنْ هِشَامٍ،
قَالَ أَخْبَرَنِي أَبِي قَالَ، سَمِعْتُ عَبْدَ اللهِ بْنَ جَعْفَرٍ، قَالَ
سَمِعْتُ عَلِيًّا ـ رضى الله عنه ـ يَقُولُ سَمِعْتُ النَّبِيَّ
صَلَّى اللهُ عَلَيْهِ وَسَلَّمَ يَقُولُ : «خَيْرُ نِسَائِهَا مَرْيَمُ ابْنَةُ
عِمْرَانَ، وَخَيْرُ نِسَائِهَا خَدِيجَةُ».

(Sayyiduna) Ali b. Abi Talib, Allah be pleased with
him, narrated: I heard the Prophet ﷺ saying,
"Maryam, the daughter of 'Imran, was the best
among the women (of her time) and Khadijah is the
best amongst the women (of her time)."[2]

---

2   Sahih al-Bukhari – Sahih Hadith

Hadith 3

حَدَّثَنَا أَبُو بَكْرِ بْنُ زَنْجُوَيْهْ، حَدَّثَنَا عَبْدُ الرَّزَّاقِ، أَخْبَرَنَا مَعْمَرٌ، عَنْ قَتَادَةَ، عَنْ أَنَسٍ، رضى الله عنه أَنَّ النَّبِيَّ صَلَّى‌اللَّهُ‌عَلَيْهِ‌وَسَلَّمَ قَالَ : «حَسْبُكَ مِنْ نِسَاءِ الْعَالَمِينَ مَرْيَمُ ابْنَةُ عِمْرَانَ وَخَدِيجَةُ بِنْتُ خُوَيْلِدٍ وَفَاطِمَةُ بِنْتُ مُحَمَّدٍ وَآسِيَةُ امْرَأَةُ فِرْعَوْنَ» .

Anas b. Malik, Allah be pleased with him, narrated that the Prophet ﷺ said: "Sufficient for you among the women of mankind are Maryam, the daughter of 'Imran, Khadijah, the daughter of Khuwaylid, Fatimah, the daughter of Muhammad and Asiyah the wife of the Pharaoh."[3]

---

3 Sunan al-Tirmidhi – Sahih Hadith

Hadith 4

حَدَّثَنَا نَصْرُ بْنُ عَلِيٍّ الْجَهْضَمِيُّ، حَدَّثَنَا عَلِيُّ بْنُ جَعْفَرِ

بْنِ مُحَمَّدِ بْنِ عَلِيٍّ، أَخْبَرَنِي أَخِي، مُوسَى بْنُ جَعْفَرِ بْنِ

مُحَمَّدٍ عَنْ أَبِيهِ، جَعْفَرِ بْنِ مُحَمَّدٍ عَنْ أَبِيهِ، مُحَمَّدِ بْنِ

عَلِيٍّ عَنْ أَبِيهِ، عَلِيِّ بْنِ الْحُسَيْنِ عَنْ أَبِيهِ، عَنْ جَدِّهِ،

عَلِيِّ بْنِ أَبِي طَالِبٍ أَنَّ رَسُولَ اللَّهِ صَلَّى اللَّهُ عَلَيْهِ وَسَلَّمَ أَخَذَ

بِيَدِ حَسَنٍ وَحُسَيْنٍ فَقَالَ «مَنْ أَحَبَّنِي وَأَحَبَّ هَذَيْنِ

وَأَبَاهُمَا وَأُمَّهُمَا كَانَ مَعِي فِي دَرَجَتِي يَوْمَ الْقِيَامَةِ».

Ali b. Husayn (known as Imam Zayn al-Abidin), narrated on the authority of his father al-Husayn, from his grandfather, Ali b. Abi Talib, Allah be pleased with them: "The Prophet ﷺ took (Imams) al-Hasan and al-Husayn by the hand and said: 'Whoever loves me and loves these two, and their father and mother, he shall be alongside me on my level on the Day of Judgement."[4]

---

4   Sunan al-Tirmidhi – Sahih Hadith

Hadith 5

حَدَّثَنَا أَبُو الْوَلِيدِ، حَدَّثَنَا ابْنُ عُيَيْنَةَ، عَنْ عَمْرِو بْنِ دِينَارٍ، عَنِ ابْنِ أَبِي مُلَيْكَةَ، عَنِ الْمِسْوَرِ بْنِ مَخْرَمَةَ، أَنَّ رَسُولَ اللهِ صَلَّى اللَّهُ عَلَيْهِ وَسَلَّمَ قَالَ : «فَاطِمَةُ بَضْعَةٌ مِنِّي، فَمَنْ أَغْضَبَهَا أَغْضَبَنِي».

al-Miswar b. Makhrama, Allah be pleased with him, narrated that the Messenger of Allah ﷺ said, "Fatimah is a part of me, and the one who makes her angry, makes me angry."[5]

---

5   Sahih al-Bukhari – Sahih Hadith

Hadith 6

حَدَّثَنِي عَنْ مَالِكٍ، عَنْ جَعْفَرِ بْنِ مُحَمَّدٍ، عَنْ أَبِيهِ،
أَنَّهُ قَالَ وَزَنَتْ فَاطِمَةُ بِنْتُ رَسُولِ اللهِ صَلَّى ٱللَّهُ عَلَيْهِ وَسَلَّمَ
شَعَرَ حَسَنٍ وَحُسَيْنٍ وَزَيْنَبَ وَأُمِّ كُلْثُومٍ فَتَصَدَّقَتْ
بِزِنَةِ ذَلِكَ فِضَّةً .

Yahya related to me from Malik from Jafar b.
Muhammad (known as Imam Jafar al-Sadiq) that his
father said, "Fatimah, the daughter of the Messenger
of Allah ﷺ weighed the hair of (Imams) al-
Hasan, al-Husayn, Zaynab, and Umm Kulthum
(Allah be pleased with them), and gave away in
charity [Sadaqah] its equivalent weight in silver."[6]

---

6   Muwatta of Imam Malik b. Anas - Sahih Hadith

Hadith 7

حَدَّثَنِي إِبْرَاهِيمُ بْنُ مُوسَى، أَخْبَرَنَا هِشَامُ بْنُ يُوسُفَ، عَنْ مَعْمَرٍ، عَنِ الزُّهْرِيِّ، عَنْ أَنَسٍ، قَالَ «لَمْ يَكُنْ أَحَدٌ أَشْبَهَ بِالنَّبِيِّ ﷺ مِنَ الْحَسَنِ بْنِ عَلِيٍّ.»

Anas b. Malik, Allah be pleased with him, said:
"None resembled the Prophet ﷺ more than
al-Hasan the son of Ali did (Allah be well pleased
with them)."[7]

---

7 Sahih al-Bukhari – Sahih Hadith

Hadith 8

أَخْبَرَنَا وَاصِلُ بْنُ عَبْدِ الْأَعْلَى قَالَ حَدَّثَنَا وَكِيعٌ عَنْ الْأَعْمَشِ عَنْ عَدِيِّ بْنِ ثَابِتٍ عَنْ زِرِّ بْنِ حُبَيْشٍ عَنْ عَلِيٍّ قَالَ عَهِدَ إِلَيَّ رَسُولُ اللَّهِ صَلَّى ٱللَّهُ عَلَيْهِ وَسَلَّمَ أَنْ لَا يُحِبُّنِي إِلَّا مُؤْمِنٌ وَلَا يَبْغُضُنِي إِلَّا مُنَافِقٌ.

It was narrated that Ali b. Abi Talib, Allah be pleased with him, said: "The Prophet ﷺ made a covenant with me that none would love me but a believer, and none would hate me but a hypocrite."[8]

---

8   Sunan al-Nasa'i – Sahih Hadith

Hadith 9

حَدَّثَنَا قُتَيْبَةُ، حَدَّثَنَا جَعْفَرُ بْنُ سُلَيْمَانَ، عَنْ أَبِي
هَارُونَ الْعَبْدِيِّ، عَنْ أَبِي سَعِيدٍ الْخُدْرِيِّ، قَالَ إِنَّا كُنَّا
لَنَعْرِفُ الْمُنَافِقِينَ نَحْنُ مَعْشَرَ الْأَنْصَارِ بِبُغْضِهِمْ عَلِيَّ
بْنَ أَبِي طَالِبٍ.

Abu Sa'id al-Khudri, Allah be pleased with him,
narrated: "We, the helpers of Madinah [Ansar], used
to recognize the hypocrites by their hatred for Ali b.
Abi Talib, Allah be pleased with him."9

---

9   Sunan al-Tirmidhi – Weak Hadith strengthened by other
    narrations

Hadith 10

حَدَّثَنَا سُفْيَانُ بْنُ وَكِيعٍ، حَدَّثَنَا أَبِي، عَنْ إِسْرَائِيلَ،
وَحَدَّثَنَا مُحَمَّدُ بْنُ إِسْمَاعِيلَ، حَدَّثَنَا عُبَيْدُ اللَّهِ بْنُ
مُوسَى، عَنْ إِسْرَائِيلَ، عَنْ أَبِي إِسْحَاقَ، عَنِ الْبَرَاءِ بْنِ
عَازِبٍ، أَنَّ النَّبِيَّ ﷺ قَالَ لِعَلِيِّ بْنِ أَبِي
طَالِبٍ : «أَنْتَ مِنِّي وَأَنَا مِنْكَ».

al-Bara b. Azib, Allah be pleased with him, narrated
that the Prophet ﷺ said to Ali b. Abi Talib,
Allah be pleased with him: "You are from me, and I
am from you."[10]

---

10 Sunan al-Tirmidhi – Sahih Hadith

Hadith 11

حَدَّثَنَا مَحْمُودُ بْنُ غَيْلاَنَ، حَدَّثَنَا أَبُو أُسَامَةَ، عَنْ

فُضَيْلِ بْنِ مَرْزُوقٍ، عَنْ عَدِيِّ بْنِ ثَابِتٍ، عَنِ الْبَرَاءِ،

أَنَّ النَّبِيَّ صَلَّى اللهُ عَلَيْهِ وَسَلَّمَ أَبْصَرَ حَسَنًا وَحُسَيْنًا فَقَالَ :

«اللَّهُمَّ إِنِّي أُحِبُّهُمَا فَأَحِبَّهُمَا».

al-Bara b. Azib, Allah be pleased with him, narrated
that the Prophet صَلَّى اللهُ عَلَيْهِ وَسَلَّمَ observed (Imams) al-
Hasan and al-Husayn, Allah be pleased with them,
and then he said: "O Allah, I love them, so love them
as well." [11]

---

11 Sunan al-Tirmidhi – Sahih Hadith

Hadith 12

حَدَّثَنَا مُحَمَّدُ بْنُ مُوسَى الْوَاسِطِيُّ، حَدَّثَنَا الْمُعَلَّى بْنُ عَبْدِ الرَّحْمَنِ، حَدَّثَنَا ابْنُ أَبِي ذِئْبٍ، عَنْ نَافِعٍ، عَنِ ابْنِ عُمَرَ، قَالَ قَالَ رَسُولُ اللهِ صَلَّى‌اللَّهُ‌عَلَيْهِ‌وَسَلَّمَ : «الْحَسَنُ وَالْحُسَيْنُ سَيِّدَا شَبَابِ أَهْلِ الْجَنَّةِ وَأَبُوهُمَا خَيْرٌ مِنْهُمَا».

It was narrated that Abdullah b. Umar, Allah be pleased with him, said: "The Messenger of Allah ﷺ said: 'al-Hasan and al-Husayn, Allah be pleased with them, will be the leaders of the youth of Paradise, and their father is better than both of them."[12]

---

12 Sunan b. Majah – Hasan Hadith

Hadith 13

حَدَّثَنِي خَلَفُ بْنُ خَالِدٍ الْقُرَشِيُّ، حَدَّثَنَا بَكْرُ بْنُ
مُضَرَ، عَنْ جَعْفَرِ بْنِ رَبِيعَةَ، عَنْ عِرَاكِ بْنِ مَالِكٍ،
عَنْ عُبَيْدِ اللَّهِ بْنِ عَبْدِ اللَّهِ بْنِ مَسْعُودٍ، عَنِ ابْنِ
عَبَّاسٍ ـ رضى الله عنهما أَنَّ الْقَمَرَ، انْشَقَّ فِي زَمَانِ
النَّبِيِّ صَلَّى ٱللَّهُ عَلَيْهِ وَسَلَّمَ .

Abdullah b. Abbas, Allah be pleased with him,
narrated: "The moon was split into two parts during
the lifetime of the Prophet ﷺ."[13]

---

13 Sahih al-Bukhari – Sahih Hadith

Hadith 14

حَدَّثَنَا مُسَدَّدٌ، حَدَّثَنَا أَبُو مُعَاوِيَةَ، مُحَمَّدُ بْنُ خَازِمٍ عَنِ الْأَعْمَشِ، عَنِ الْحَسَنِ بْنِ عَمْرٍو، عَنْ مِهْرَانَ أَبِي صَفْوَانَ، عَنِ ابْنِ عَبَّاسٍ، قَالَ قَالَ رَسُولُ اللهِ صَلَّى اللَّهُ عَلَيْهِ وَسَلَّمَ : «مَنْ أَرَادَ الْحَجَّ فَلْيَتَعَجَّلْ» .

Abdullah b. Abbas, Allah be pleased with him, narrated that the Prophet ﷺ said: "He who intends to perform the great pilgrimage to Mecca [Hajj] should hasten to do so."[14]

---

14 Sunan Abu Dawud – Hasan Hadith

Hadith 15

أَخْبَرَنَا عِيسَى بْنُ حَمَّادٍ، قَالَ أَنْبَأَنَا اللَّيْثُ، عَنْ يَزِيدَ
بْنِ أَبِي حَبِيبٍ، عَنِ ابْنِ أَبِي الصَّعْبَةِ، عَنْ رَجُلٍ، مِنْ
هَمْدَانَ يُقَالُ لَهُ أَبُو أَفْلَحَ عَنِ ابْنِ زُرَيْرٍ، أَنَّهُ سَمِعَ عَلِيَّ
بْنَ أَبِي طَالِبٍ، يَقُولُ إِنَّ رَسُولَ اللهِ صَلَّى اللهُ عَلَيْهِ وَسَلَّمَ
أَخَذَ حَرِيرًا فَجَعَلَهُ فِي يَمِينِهِ وَأَخَذَ ذَهَبًا فَجَعَلَهُ فِي
شِمَالِهِ ثُمَّ قَالَ : «إِنَّ هَذَيْنِ حَرَامٌ عَلَى ذُكُورِ أُمَّتِي».

Ali b. Abi Talib, Allah be pleased with him, said:
"The Messenger of Allah صَلَّى اللهُ عَلَيْهِ وَسَلَّمَ took hold of
some silk in his right hand and some gold in his left,
then he said: 'These two are forbidden for the males
of my community [Ummah].'"[15]

---

15 Sunan al-Nasa'i – Sahih Hadith

Hadith 16

وَحَدَّثَنِي عَنْ مَالِكٍ، عَنِ ابْنِ شِهَابٍ، عَنْ عَلِيِّ بْنِ
حُسَيْنِ بْنِ عَلِيِّ بْنِ أَبِي طَالِبٍ، أَنَّ رَسُولَ اللَّهِ
صَلَّى اللَّهُ عَلَيْهِ وَسَلَّمَ قَالَ : «مِنْ حُسْنِ إِسْلَامِ الْمَرْءِ تَرْكُهُ مَا
لَا يَعْنِيهِ».

Yahya related to me from Malik from Ibn Shihab
(known as Imam Zuhri) from Ali b. Husayn (known
as Imam Zayn al-Abidin) b. Ali b. Abi Talib, Allah
be pleased with them, that the Messenger of Allah
ﷺ said, "Part of the excellence of an
individual's Islam is that they leave that which does
not concern them."[16]

---

16 Muwatta of Imam Malik b. Anas – Sahih Hadith

Hadith 17

حَدَّثَنَا قُتَيْبَةُ، وَهَنَّادٌ، وَمَحْمُودُ بْنُ غَيْلاَنَ، قَالُوا حَدَّثَنَا
وَكِيعٌ، عَنْ سُفْيَانَ، وَحَدَّثَنَا مُحَمَّدُ بْنُ بَشَّارٍ، حَدَّثَنَا
عَبْدُ الرَّحْمَنِ بْنُ مَهْدِيٍّ، حَدَّثَنَا سُفْيَانُ، عَنْ عَبْدِ اللَّهِ
بْنِ مُحَمَّدِ بْنِ عَقِيلٍ، عَنْ مُحَمَّدِ ابْنِ الْحَنَفِيَّةِ، عَنْ عَلِيٍّ،
عَنِ النَّبِيِّ ﷺ قَالَ : «مِفْتَاحُ الصَّلاَةِ
الطُّهُورُ وَتَحْرِيمُهَا التَّكْبِيرُ وَتَحْلِيلُهَا التَّسْلِيمُ».

Ali b. Abi Talib, Allah be pleased with him, narrated that the Prophet ﷺ said: "The key to prayer [Salat] is purification, its entrance is the Takbir, and its exit is upon the sending of salutations [Taslim]."[17]

---

17 Sunan al-Tirmidhi – Hasan Hadith

Hadith 18

حَدَّثَنَا قُتَيْبَةُ، حَدَّثَنَا بَكْرُ بْنُ مُضَرَ، عَنِ ابْنِ الْهَادِ، عَنْ مُحَمَّدِ بْنِ إِبْرَاهِيمَ، عَنْ عَامِرِ بْنِ سَعْدِ بْنِ أَبِي وَقَّاصٍ، عَنِ الْعَبَّاسِ بْنِ عَبْدِ الْمُطَّلِبِ، أَنَّهُ سَمِعَ رَسُولَ اللَّهِ صَلَّى اللَّهُ عَلَيْهِ وَسَلَّمَ يَقُولُ : «إِذَا سَجَدَ الْعَبْدُ سَجَدَ مَعَهُ سَبْعَةُ آرَابٍ وَجْهُهُ وَكَفَّاهُ وَرُكْبَتَاهُ وَقَدَمَاهُ».

al-Abbas b. Abdul-Muttalib, Allah be pleased with him, narrated that he heard the Messenger of Allah صَلَّى اللَّهُ عَلَيْهِ وَسَلَّمَ saying: "When the servant prostrates; his face, hands, knees, and feet (prostrate with him)."[18]

---

18 Sunan al-Tirmidhi – Sahih Hadith

Hadith 19

حَدَّثَنَا قُتَيْبَةُ بْنُ سَعِيدٍ، حَدَّثَنَا بَكْرٌ، - وَهُوَ ابْنُ مُضَرَ - عَنِ ابْنِ الْهَادِ، عَنْ مُحَمَّدِ بْنِ إِبْرَاهِيمَ، عَنْ عَامِرِ بْنِ سَعْدٍ، عَنِ الْعَبَّاسِ بْنِ عَبْدِ الْمُطَّلِبِ، أَنَّهُ سَمِعَ رَسُولَ اللَّهِ صَلَّى اللَّهُ عَلَيْهِ وَسَلَّمَ يَقُولُ : ‹‹إِذَا سَجَدَ الْعَبْدُ سَجَدَ مَعَهُ سَبْعَةُ أَطْرَافٍ وَجْهُهُ وَكَفَّاهُ وَرُكْبَتَاهُ وَقَدَمَاهُ››.

It was narrated from al-Abbas b. Abdul Muttalib, Allah be pleased with him, that he heard the Messenger of Allah ﷺ say: "When a person is in a state of prostration, he prostrates on seven parts of the body: His face, his hands, his knees, and his feet."[19]

---

19 Sahih Muslim – Sahih Hadith

Hadith 20

حَدَّثَنَا قُتَيْبَةُ، حَدَّثَنَا اللَّيْثُ، عَنِ ابْنِ الْهَادِ، عَنْ
مُحَمَّدِ بْنِ إِبْرَاهِيمَ بْنِ الْحَارِثِ، عَنْ عَامِرِ بْنِ سَعْدِ بْنِ
أَبِي وَقَّاصٍ، عَنِ الْعَبَّاسِ بْنِ عَبْدِ الْمُطَّلِبِ، أَنَّهُ سَمِعَ
رَسُولَ اللَّهِ ﷺ يَقُولُ : «ذَاقَ طَعْمَ الإِيمَانِ
مَنْ رَضِيَ بِاللَّهِ رَبًّا وَبِالإِسْلاَم دِينًا وَبِمُحَمَّدٍ نَبِيًّا».

al-Abbas b. Abdul-Muttalib, Allah be pleased with
him, narrated that he heard the Messenger of Allah
ﷺ say: "Whoever is pleased with Allah as
their Lord, and Islam as their way of life, and
Muhammad ﷺ as their Prophet, then they
have tasted the sweetness of faith."

Hadith 21

حَدَّثَنَا مُحَمَّدُ بْنُ الْمُؤَمَّلِ بْنِ الصَّبَّاحِ، وَعَبَّادُ بْنُ الْوَلِيدِ، قَالاَ حَدَّثَنَا بَكْرُ بْنُ يَحْيَى بْنِ زَبَّانَ، حَدَّثَنَا حِبَّانُ بْنُ عَلِيٍّ، عَنْ يَزِيدَ بْنِ أَبِي زِيَادٍ، عَنْ عَبْدِ اللَّهِ بْنِ مُحَمَّدِ بْنِ عَقِيلِ بْنِ أَبِي طَالِبٍ، عَنْ أَبِيهِ، عَنْ جَدِّهِ، قَالَ قَالَ رَسُولُ اللَّهِ ـ صلى الله عليه وسلم : " يُجْزِئُ مِنَ الْوُضُوءِ مُدٌّ وَمِنَ الْغُسْلِ صَاعٌ " . فَقَالَ رَجُلٌ لاَ يُجْزِئُنَا . فَقَالَ قَدْ كَانَ يُجْزِئُ مَنْ هُوَ خَيْرٌ مِنْكَ وَأَكْثَرُ شَعَرًا . يَعْنِي النَّبِيَّ صَلَّى‌اللَّهُ‌عَلَيْهِ‌وَسَلَّمَ .

Abdullah b. Muhammad b. Aqil b. Abi Talib narrated from his father that his grandfather, Allah be pleased with them, said: "The Messenger of Allah ﷺ said: 'A Mudd is sufficient for the one performing ablution and a Sa' is sufficient in regards to performing ghusl.' A man said: 'Well, it's not sufficient for us!'" He (the narrator) said: "It was sufficient for one who is better than you and had more hair!", meaning the Prophet.[20]

(One Mudd is approximately .75 liters and One Sa' is approximately 3 liters)

---

20 Sunan b. Majah – Sahih Hadith

Hadith 22

حَدَّثَنَا مُحَمَّدُ بْنُ يَحْيَى، حَدَّثَنَا دَاوُدُ بْنُ شَبِيبٍ،
حَدَّثَنَا حَبِيبُ بْنُ أَبِي حَبِيبٍ، عَنْ عَمْرِو بْنِ هَرَمٍ،
عَنْ عِكْرِمَةَ، عَنْ عَائِشَةَ، عَنِ النَّبِيِّ صَلَّى اللهُ عَلَيْهِ وَسَلَّمَ
أَنَّهُمَا كَانَا يَتَوَضَّآنِ جَمِيعًا لِلصَّلاَةِ .

It was narrated from (the mother of the believers) -
Aisha, Allah be pleased with her, that the Prophet
صَلَّى اللهُ عَلَيْهِ وَسَلَّمَ and she used to perform ablution together
for prayer.[21]

---

21 Sunan b. Majah – Sahih Hadith

Hadith 23

أَخْبَرَنَا عَمْرُو بْنُ عَلِيٍّ، قَالَ حَدَّثَنَا يَحْيَى بْنُ سَعِيدٍ،
قَالَ حَدَّثَنَا حَمَّادُ بْنُ زَيْدٍ، قَالَ حَدَّثَنَا غَيْلَانُ بْنُ
جَرِيرٍ، عَنْ مُطَرِّفِ بْنِ عَبْدِ اللَّهِ، قَالَ صَلَّى عَلِيُّ بْنُ
أَبِي طَالِبٍ فَكَانَ يُكَبِّرُ فِي كُلِّ خَفْضٍ وَرَفْعٍ يُتِمُّ
التَّكْبِيرَ. فَقَالَ عِمْرَانُ بْنُ حُصَيْنٍ لَقَدْ ذَكَّرَنِي هَذَا
صَلَاةَ رَسُولِ اللَّهِ صَلَّى اللَّهُ عَلَيْهِ وَسَلَّمَ.

Mutarrif b. Abdullahi, narrated: "When Ali b. Abi
Talib prayed, Allah be pleased with him, every time
he went down into the bowing position [Ruku], and
then came up from it, within all movements of the
prayer in general, he would say the Takbir."

Imran b. Husayn said: "This reminds me of the
prayer of the Messenger of Allah ﷺ."[22]

---

22 Sahih al-Bukhari – Sahih Hadith

Hadith 24

حَدَّثَنَا زِيَادُ بْنُ أَيُّوبَ الْبَغْدَادِيُّ، حَدَّثَنَا أَبُو تُمَيْلَةَ، عَنْ عَبْدِ الْمُؤْمِنِ بْنِ خَالِدٍ، عَنْ عَبْدِ اللهِ بْنِ بُرَيْدَةَ، عَنْ أُمِّهِ، عَنْ أُمِّ سَلَمَةَ، قَالَتْ كَانَ أَحَبُّ الثِّيَابِ إِلَى النَّبِيِّ صَلَّى اللهُ عَلَيْهِ وَسَلَّمَ الْقَمِيصُ .

The mother of the believers, Umm Salamah, Allah be pleased with her, said: "The most beloved garment to the Messenger of Allah ﷺ was the long shirt [Qamis]."[23]

---

23 Sunan al-Tirmidhi – Hasan/Good Hadith

Hadith 25

أَخْبَرَنَا يَعْقُوبُ بْنُ إِبْرَاهِيمَ، قَالَ حَدَّثَنَا ابْنُ عُلَيَّةَ، عَنْ أَيُّوبَ، عَنْ عَبْدِ اللَّهِ بْنِ سَعِيدِ بْنِ جُبَيْرٍ، عَنْ أَبِيهِ، عَنِ ابْنِ عَبَّاسٍ، قَالَ بِتُّ عِنْدَ خَالَتِي مَيْمُونَةَ فَقَامَ رَسُولُ اللَّهِ صلى الله عليه وسلم يُصَلِّي مِنَ اللَّيْلِ فَقُمْتُ عَنْ شِمَالِهِ فَقَالَ بِي هَكَذَا فَأَخَذَ بِرَأْسِي فَأَقَامَنِي عَنْ يَمِينِهِ .

It was narrated that Abdullah b. Abbas, Allah be pleased with him, said: "I stayed overnight with my maternal aunt, the mother of the believers, Maymunah, Allah be pleased with her, and the Messenger of Allah ﷺ got up to pray at night (to pray Tahajud). I stood on his left, so he gestured tome, meaning, he took me by the head and made me stand on his right."[24]

---

24 Sunan al-Nasa'i – Sahih Hadith

Hadith 26

حَدَّثَنَا أَبُو إِسْحَاق الشَّافِعِيُّ، إِبْرَاهِيمُ بْنُ مُحَمَّدِ بْنِ
الْعَبَّاسِ حَدَّثَنَا سُفْيَانُ، عَنْ عَمْرٍو، سَمِعَ كُرَيْبًا،
يَقُولُ سَمِعْتُ ابْنَ عَبَّاسٍ، يَقُولُ بِتُّ عِنْدَ خَالَتِي
مَيْمُونَةَ فَقَامَ النَّبِيُّ صَلَّى اللَّهُ عَلَيْهِ وَسَلَّمَ فَتَوَضَّأَ مِنْ شَنَّةٍ
وُضُوءًا يُقَلِّلُهُ فَقُمْتُ فَصَنَعْتُ كَمَا صَنَعَ .

It was narrated that Amr heard Kurayb, Allah be
pleased with him, saying: "I heard Abdullah b.
Abbas, Allah be pleased with him, say: 'I stayed
overnight with my maternal aunt Maymunah, Allah
be pleased with her, and the Prophet ﷺ got
up and performed ablution from an old water skin,
and he performed a brief ablution. Then I got up
and did the same as he had done.'"[25]

---

25 Sunan b. Majah – Sahih Hadith

Hadith 27

وَحَدَّثَنِي أَحْمَدُ بْنُ عَبْدِ اللهِ بْنِ الْحَكَمِ، حَدَّثَنَا مُحَمَّدُ بْنُ جَعْفَرٍ، حَدَّثَنَا شُعْبَةُ، عَنْ زَيْدِ بْنِ مُحَمَّدٍ، قَالَ سَمِعْتُ نَافِعًا، يُحَدِّثُ عَنِ ابْنِ عُمَرَ، عَنْ حَفْصَةَ، قَالَتْ كَانَ رَسُولُ اللهِ صَلَّى‌اللهُ‌عَلَيْهِ‌وَسَلَّمَ إِذَا طَلَعَ الْفَجْرُ لاَ يُصَلِّي إِلاَّ رَكْعَتَيْنِ خَفِيفَتَيْنِ.

(The mother of the believers) - Hafsa, Allah be pleased with her, reported: "When it was dawn, the Messenger of Allah ﷺ did not observe (any other prayers) other than two short cycles of prayers [Rakats]." [26]

---

26 Sahih Muslim – Sahih Hadith

Hadith 28

أَخْبَرَنَا مُحَمَّدُ بْنُ عَبْدِ اللهِ بْنِ الْمُبَارَكِ، قَالَ حَدَّثَنَا سُلَيْمَانُ بْنُ حَرْبٍ، وَهِشَامُ بْنُ عَبْدِ الْمَلِكِ، قَالَا حَدَّثَنَا حَمَّادُ بْنُ سَلَمَةَ، عَنْ هِشَامٍ بْنِ عَمْرٍو الْفَزَارِيِّ، عَنْ عَبْدِ الرَّحْمَنِ بْنِ الْحَارِثِ بْنِ هِشَامٍ، عَنْ عَلِيِّ بْنِ أَبِي طَالِبٍ، أَنَّ النَّبِيَّ ﷺ كَانَ يَقُولُ فِي آخِرِ وِتْرِهِ " اللَّهُمَّ إِنِّي أَعُوذُ بِرِضَاكَ مِنْ سَخَطِكَ وَبِمُعَافَاتِكَ مِنْ عُقُوبَتِكَ وَأَعُوذُ بِكَ مِنْكَ لاَ أُحْصِي ثَنَاءً عَلَيْكَ أَنْتَ كَمَا أَثْنَيْتَ عَلَى نَفْسِكَ " .

It was narrated from Ali b. Abi Talib: The Prophet ﷺ used to say at the end of the Witr prayer: "O Allah, I seek refuge in Your pleasure from Your wrath and in Your forgiveness from Your punishment. I seek refuge in You from You; I cannot praise You enough; You are as You have praised

Yourself."[27]

27 Sunan al-Nasa'i – Sahih Hadith

Hadith 29

أَخْبَرَنَا إِبْرَاهِيمُ بْنُ هَارُونَ، قَالَ حَدَّثَنَا حَاتِمُ بْنُ
إِسْمَاعِيلَ، قَالَ حَدَّثَنَا جَعْفَرُ بْنُ مُحَمَّدِ بْنِ عَلِيِّ بْنِ
الْحُسَيْنِ، عَنْ أَبِيهِ، أَنَّ جَابِرَ بْنَ عَبْدِ اللَّهِ، قَالَ صَلَّى
رَسُولُ اللَّهِ صَلَّى اللَّهُ عَلَيْهِ وَسَلَّمَ الصُّبْحَ حِينَ تَبَيَّنَ لَهُ الصُّبْحُ

.

Imam Jafar b. Muhammad b. narrated from (Imam
Zayn al-Abidin) - Ali the son of (Imam) al-Husayn
narrated from his father, that Jabir b. Abdullah said:
"The Messenger of Allah ﷺ prayed the dawn
prayer [Subh] as soon as he was certain the dawn
had appeared."[28]

---

28 Sunan al-Nasa'i – Sahih Hadith

Hadith 30

أَخْبَرَنِي إِبْرَاهِيمُ بْنُ هَارُونَ، قَالَ حَدَّثَنَا حَاتِمُ بْنُ
إِسْمَاعِيلَ، قَالَ حَدَّثَنَا جَعْفَرُ بْنُ مُحَمَّدِ بْنِ عَلِيِّ بْنِ
حُسَيْنٍ، عَنْ أَبِيهِ، قَالَ دَخَلْنَا عَلَى جَابِرِ بْنِ عَبْدِ اللَّهِ
فَقُلْتُ أَخْبِرْنِي عَنْ حَجَّةِ النَّبِيِّ، صلى الله عليه وسلم
. فَقَالَ إِنَّ رَسُولَ اللَّهِ ﷺ رَمَى الْجَمْرَةَ الَّتِي عِنْدَ
الشَّجَرَةِ بِسَبْعِ حَصَيَاتٍ يُكَبِّرُ مَعَ كُلِّ حَصَاةٍ مِنْهَا
حَصَى الْخَذْفِ رَمَى مِنْ بَطْنِ الْوَادِي ثُمَّ انْصَرَفَ إِلَى
الْمَنْحَرِ فَنَحَرَ .

Jafar b. Muhammad b. Ali b. al-Husayn narrated
that his father said: "We entered upon Jabir b.
Abdullah and I said: 'Tell me about the Hajj of the
Prophet. He said: 'The Messenger of Allah stoned
the Jamarat which is by the tree, with seven pebbles,
saying the Takbir – Allahu Akbar – with each pebble
- pebbles that were the size of date stones or

fingertips. And he threw them from the bottom of the valley, then he went to the place of sacrifice in Mina."[29]

---

29 Sunan al-Nasa'i – Sahih Hadith

Hadith 31

حَدَّثَنَا قُتَيْبَةُ، حَدَّثَنَا هُشَيْمٌ، عَنْ مَنْصُورِ بْنِ زَاذَانَ،
عَنِ ابْنِ سِيرِينَ، عَنِ ابْنِ عَبَّاسٍ، أَنَّ النَّبِيَّ ﷺ خَرَجَ
مِنَ الْمَدِينَةِ إِلَى مَكَّةَ لاَ يَخَافُ إِلاَّ اللَّهَ رَبَّ الْعَالَمِينَ
فَصَلَّى رَكْعَتَيْنِ .

Abdullah b. Abbas, Allah be pleased with him,
narrated: "The Prophet ﷺ went from the
city of Madinah to Mecca, not fearing anyone except
Allah the Lord of the worlds, and he prayed two
cycles of prayer [2 Rakat]."[30]

---

30 Sunan al-Tirmidhi – Sahih Hadith

Hadith 32

حَدَّثَنِي يَحْيَى، عَنْ مَالِكٍ، عَنْ جَعْفَرِ بْنِ مُحَمَّدٍ، عَنْ
أَبِيهِ، عَنْ جَابِرِ بْنِ عَبْدِ اللَّهِ، أَنَّهُ قَالَ رَأَيْتُ رَسُولَ
اللَّهِ صَلَّى اللَّهُ عَلَيْهِ وَسَلَّمَ رَمَلَ مِنَ الْحَجَرِ الْأَسْوَدِ حَتَّى
انْتَهَى إِلَيْهِ ثَلاَثَةَ أَطْوَافٍ .

Yahya related to me from Malik from Jafar b.
Muhammad from his father that Jabir b. Abdullah
said, "I saw the Messenger of Allah, ﷺ
hastening from the Black Stone (at the Kaba in
Mecca) until he reached it again, three times."

Imam Malik b. Anas, said, "This is what is still done
by the people of knowledge in our city."[31]

---

31 Muwatta of Imam Malik b. Anas – Sahih Hadith

Hadith 33

حَدَّثَنَا سَعِيدُ بْنُ سُلَيْمَانَ، قَالَ: حَدَّثَنَا مُبَارَكُ، عَنْ
ثَابِتٍ، عَنْ أَنَسٍ قَالَ: كَانَ النَّبِيُّ صَلَّى اللهُ عَلَيْهِ وَسَلَّمَ إِذَا أُتِيَ
بِالشَّيْءِ يَقُولُ: اذْهَبُوا بِهِ إِلَى فُلَانَةٍ، فَإِنَّهَا كَانَتْ
صَدِيقَةَ خَدِيجَةَ. اذْهَبُوا بِهِ إِلَى بَيْتِ فُلَانَةٍ، فَإِنَّهَا
كَانَتْ تُحِبُّ خَدِيجَةَ.

Anas b. Malik, Allah be pleased with him, said,
"When the Prophet ﷺ was given something,
he used to say, 'Take it to so-and-so, she was a friend
of Khadijah. Take it to the house of so-and-so, she
loved Khadijah.'"[32]

---

32 al-Adab al-Mufrad of Imam al-Bukhari – Hasan/Good
Hadith

Hadith 34

حَدَّثَنَا قُتَيْبَةُ، حَدَّثَنَا عَبْدُ الْوَاحِدِ بْنُ زِيَادٍ، عَنْ عَبْدِ
الرَّحْمَنِ بْنِ إِسْحَاقَ، عَنِ النُّعْمَانِ بْنِ سَعْدٍ، عَنْ عَلِيِّ
بْنِ أَبِي طَالِبٍ، قَالَ قَالَ رَسُولُ اللهِ صَلَّى اللَّهُ عَلَيْهِ وَسَلَّمَ : "
خَيْرُكُمْ مَنْ تَعَلَّمَ الْقُرْآنَ وَعَلَّمَهُ "

Ali b. Abi Talib, Allah be pleased with him, narrated
that the Messenger of Allah صَلَّى اللَّهُ عَلَيْهِ وَسَلَّمَ said: "The
best of you is he who learns the Quran and then
teaches it."[33]

---

33 Sunan al-Tirmidhi – Sahih Hadith

Hadith 35

حَدَّثَنَا مُحَمَّدُ بْنُ يَحْيَى، حَدَّثَنَا أَزْهَرُ السَّمَّانُ، عَنِ ابْنِ
عَوْنٍ، عَنْ مُحَمَّدٍ، عَنْ عَبِيدَةَ، عَنْ عَلِيٍّ، رضى الله
عنه قَالَ جَاءَتْ فَاطِمَةُ إِلَى النَّبِيِّ صَلَّى اللَّهُ عَلَيْهِ وَسَلَّمَ تَشْكُو
مَجَلاً بِيَدَيْهَا فَأَمَرَهَا بِالتَّسْبِيحِ وَالتَّكْبِيرِ وَالتَّحْمِيدِ .

Ali b. Abi Talib, Allah be pleased with him, said:
"Fatimah, Allah be pleased with her, went to the
Prophet complaining of her hands blistering, so he
ordered her to say (SubhanAllah) Tasbih, (Allahu
Akbar) Takbir, and (Alhamdulillah) Tahmid."[34]

---

34 Sunan al-Tirmidhi – Sahih Hadith

Hadith 36

حَدَّثَنَا عَبْدُ اللَّهِ بْنُ أَبِي زِيَادٍ، حَدَّثَنَا أَبُو نُبَاتَةَ، يُونُسُ
بْنُ يَحْيَى بْنِ نُبَاتَةَ حَدَّثَنَا سَلَمَةُ بْنُ وَرْدَانَ، عَنْ أَبِي
سَعِيدِ بْنِ الْمُعَلَّى، عَنْ عَلِيِّ بْنِ أَبِي طَالِبٍ، وَأَبِي، هُرَيْرَةَ
رضى الله عنهما قَالاَ قَالَ رَسُولُ اللَّهِ صَلَّى اللَّهُ عَلَيْهِ وَسَلَّمَ "
مَا بَيْنَ بَيْتِي وَمِنْبَرِي رَوْضَةٌ مِنْ رِيَاضِ الْجَنَّةِ "

Ali b. Abi Talib and Abu Hurayrah, Allah be pleased
with them, narrated that the Messenger of Allah
ﷺ said: "Whatever is between my house and
my pulpit is a garden from the gardens of
Paradise."[35]

---

35 Sunan al-Tirmidhi – Sahih Hadith

Hadith 37

أَخْبَرَنَا إِسْمَاعِيلُ بْنُ مَسْعُودٍ، عَنْ يَزِيدَ، - وَهُوَ ابْنُ زُرَيْعٍ - قَالَ : حَدَّثَنَا شُعْبَةُ، عَنْ أَبِي جَمْرَةَ، عَنِ ابْنِ عَبَّاسٍ، قَالَ : جُعِلَ تَحْتَ رَسُولِ اللهِ صَلَّى اللَّهُ عَلَيْهِ وَسَلَّمَ حِينَ دُفِنَ قَطِيفَةٌ حَمْرَاءُ .

It was narrated that Abdullah b. Abbas said: "When the Messenger of Allah ﷺ was buried, a red velvet cloak was placed beneath him."[36]

---

36 Sunan al-Nasa'i – Sahih Hadith

Hadith 38

حَدَّثَنَا أَحْمَدُ بْنُ عَبْدَةَ الضَّبِّيُّ، وَعَلِيُّ بْنُ حُجْرٍ، وَغَيْرُ وَاحِدٍ، قَالُوا: حَدَّثَنَا عِيسَى بْنُ يُونُسَ، عَنْ عُمَرَ بْنِ عَبْدِ اللهِ مَوْلَى غُفْرَةَ، قَالَ: حَدَّثَنِي إِبْرَاهِيمُ بْنُ مُحَمَّدٍ مِنْ وَلَدِ عَلِيِّ بْنِ أَبِي طَالِبٍ، قَالَ: كَانَ عَلِيٌّ، إِذَا وَصَفَ رَسُولَ اللهِ صَلَّى‏اللَّهُ‏عَلَيْهِ‏وَسَلَّمَ فَذَكَرَ الْحَدِيثَ بِطُولِهِ، وَقَالَ: بَيْنَ كَتِفَيْهِ خَاتَمُ النُّبُوَّةِ، وَهُوَ خَاتَمُ النَّبِيِّينَ.

Ibrahim b. Muhammad, who is the grandson of Ali b. Abi Talib said: "Whenever Ali used to describe the noble attributes of the Messenger of Allah, he used to mention the complete prophetic saying[37]. He also used to say that the seal of prophethood was between his shoulders, and that the Messenger of Allah was the seal of all prophets."[38]

---

37 Hadith concerning the Hilyah Sharif
38 Shamail Muhammadiyyah of Imam al-Tirmdihi

Hadith 39

حَدَّثَنَا عَلِيُّ بْنُ الْجَعْدِ، قَالَ أَخْبَرَنَا شُعْبَةُ، قَالَ أَخْبَرَنِي
مَنْصُورٌ، قَالَ سَمِعْتُ رِبْعِيَّ بْنَ حِرَاشٍ، يَقُولُ سَمِعْتُ
عَلِيًّا، يَقُولُ قَالَ النَّبِيُّ صَلَّى اللَّهُ عَلَيْهِ وَسَلَّمَ : '' لاَ تَكْذِبُوا
عَلَيَّ، فَإِنَّهُ مَنْ كَذَبَ عَلَيَّ فَلْيَلِجِ النَّارَ ''.

Ali b. Abi Talib, Allah be pleased with him, narrated
that the Prophet ﷺ said, "Don't lie regarding
me, for whoever tells a lie on me (intentionally),
then he will most certainly enter the hell-fire."[39]

---

39 Sahih al-Bukhari – Sahih Hadith

Hadith 40

حَدَّثَنِي يَحْيَى، عَنْ مَالِكٍ، عَنْ جَعْفَرِ بْنِ مُحَمَّدٍ، عَنْ
أَبِيهِ، أَنَّ رَسُولَ اللَّهِ صَلَّى اللَّهُ عَلَيْهِ وَسَلَّمَ غُسِّلَ فِي قَمِيصٍ .

Yahya related to me from Malik from Jafar b.
Muhammad from his father, that the Messenger of
Allah, صَلَّى اللَّهُ عَلَيْهِ وَسَلَّمَ was washed (when he was taken
from this worldly life) in a long shirt.[40]

---

40 Muwatta of Imam Malik b. Anas – Sahih Hadith

Hadith 41

عَنْ أَبِيهِ عَلِيِّ بْنِ حُسَيْنٍ عَنْ أَبِيهِ أَنَّ النَّبِيَّ
صَلَّى اللَّهُ عَلَيْهِ وَسَلَّمَ قَالَ : الْبَخِيلُ مَنْ ذُكِرْتُ عِنْدَهُ ثُمَّ لَمْ
يُصَلِّ عَلَيَّ صَلَّى اللَّهُ عَلَيْهِ وَسَلَّمَ

Ali b. Husayn narrated by way of his father, Imam al-Husayn, who reported that his father Ali b. Abi Talib said: The Prophet ﷺ said, "The miser is the one in whose presence I am mentioned, and yet he does not supplicate on my behalf."[41]

---

41 Musnad of Imam Ahmad b. Hanbal – Sahih Hadith

Hadith 42

وَحَدَّثَنِي مُحَمَّدُ بْنُ رَافِعٍ، حَدَّثَنَا شَبَابَةُ، حَدَّثَنَا لَيْثٌ، عَنْ يَزِيدَ، عَنْ عِرَاكٍ، عَنْ حَفْصَةَ بِنْتِ عَبْدِ الرَّحْمَنِ بْنِ أَبِي بَكْرٍ، - وَكَانَتْ تَحْتَ الْمُنْذِرِ بْنِ الزُّبَيْرِ - أَنَّ عَائِشَةَ، أَخْبَرَتْهَا أَنَّهَا، كَانَتْ تَغْتَسِلُ هِيَ وَالنَّبِيُّ صَلَّىٰٱللّٰهُعَلَيْهِوَسَلَّمَ فِي إِنَاءٍ وَاحِدٍ يَسَعُ ثَلاَثَةَ أَمْدَادٍ أَوْ قَرِيبًا مِنْ ذَلِكَ .

Hafsa, daughter of 'Abd al-Rahman b. Abi Bakr, reported that Aisha narrated to her that she and the Messenger of Allah ﷺ "took a bath from the same vessel which contained water equal to approximately three Mudds."[42]

---

42 Sahih Muslim – Sahih Hadith

Hadith 43

حَدَّثَنَا ابْنُ أَبِي عُمَرَ، حَدَّثَنَا سُفْيَانُ بْنُ عُيَيْنَةَ، عَنْ
عَمْرِو بْنِ دِينَارٍ، عَنْ أَبِي الشَّعْثَاءِ، عَنِ ابْنِ عَبَّاسٍ،
قَالَ حَدَّثَتْنِي مَيْمُونَةُ، قَالَتْ كُنْتُ أَغْتَسِلُ أَنَا وَ رَسُولُ
اللَّهِ، صَلَّى اللَّهُ عَلَيْهِ وَسَلَّمَ مِنْ إِنَاءٍ وَاحِدٍ مِنَ الْجَنَابَةِ "

(The mother of the believers) - Maymunah, Allah be
pleased with her, said: "I and the Messenger of Allah
ﷺ would perform the major purification
bath [Ghusl] in order to remove the state of Janabah
from one vessel."[43]

---

43 Sunan al-Tirmidhi – Sahih Hadith

Hadith 44

أَخْبَرَنَا عَبْدُ الرَّحْمَنِ بْنُ إِبْرَاهِيمَ، دُحَيْمٌ قَالَ حَدَّثَنَا مَرْوَانُ بْنُ مُعَاوِيَةَ، قَالَ حَدَّثَنَا عُبَيْدُ اللَّهِ بْنُ عَبْدِ اللَّهِ بْنِ الأَصَمِّ، قَالَ حَدَّثَنِي يَزِيدُ بْنُ الأَصَمِّ، عَنْ مَيْمُونَةَ، قَالَتْ كَانَ رَسُولُ اللَّهِ صَلَّى اللَّهُ عَلَيْهِ وَسَلَّمَ إِذَا سَجَدَ خَوَّى بِيَدَيْهِ حَتَّى يُرَى وَضَحُ إِبْطَيْهِ مِنْ وَرَائِهِ وَإِذَا قَعَدَ اطْمَأَنَّ عَلَى فَخِذِهِ الْيُسْرَى .

It was narrated that Maymunah, Allah be pleased with her, said: "When the Messenger of Allah صَلَّى اللَّهُ عَلَيْهِ وَسَلَّمَ prostrated, he would hold his arms out to his sides, so that even the light area of his armpits could be seen from behind. And when he sat, he would rest on his left thigh."[44]

---

44 Sunan al-Nasa'i – Sahih Hadith

Hadith 45

أَخْبَرَنَا الْحَارِثُ بْنُ مِسْكِينٍ، قِرَاءَةً عَلَيْهِ وَأَنَا أَسْمَعُ، عَنِ ابْنِ وَهْبٍ، عَنْ يُونُسَ، وَاللَّيْثُ، عَنِ ابْنِ شِهَابٍ، عَنْ حَبِيبٍ، مَوْلَى عُرْوَةَ عَنْ بُدَيَّةَ، - وَكَانَ اللَّيْثُ يَقُولُ نَدَبَةَ - مَوْلَاةِ مَيْمُونَةَ عَنْ مَيْمُونَةَ قَالَتْ كَانَ رَسُولُ اللَّهِ صَلَّىاللَّهُعَلَيْهِوَسَلَّمَ يُبَاشِرُ الْمَرْأَةَ مِنْ نِسَائِهِ وَهِيَ حَائِضٌ إِذَا كَانَ عَلَيْهَا إِزَارٌ يَبْلُغُ أَنْصَافَ الْفَخِذَيْنِ وَالرُّكْبَتَيْنِ فِي حَدِيثِ اللَّيْثِ تَحْتَجِزُ بِهِ

It was narrated that Maymunah, Allah be pleased with her, said: "If a wife of the Messenger of Allah ﷺ was menstruating, he would fondle her, as long as she wore an Izar (waist wrap) that reached halfway down her thighs or up to her knees."[45]

---

45 Sunan al-Nasa'i – Hasan Hadith

Hadith 46

حَدَّثَنَا أَبُو بَكْرِ بْنُ أَبِي شَيْبَةَ، حَدَّثَنَا إِسْمَاعِيلُ ابْنُ عُلَيَّةَ، عَنْ هِشَامٍ الدَّسْتَوَائِيِّ، عَنْ يَحْيَى بْنِ أَبِي كَثِيرٍ، عَنْ أَبِي سَلَمَةَ، عَنْ زَيْنَبَ بِنْتِ أُمِّ سَلَمَةَ، عَنْ أُمِّ سَلَمَةَ، أَنَّهَا كَانَتْ وَرَسُولُ اللَّهِ صَلَّى اللَّهُ عَلَيْهِ وَسَلَّمَ يَغْتَسِلَانِ مِنْ إِنَاءٍ وَاحِدٍ .

Zaynab, the daughter of Umm Salamah, narrated from Umm Salamah herself that: She and the Messenger of Allah ﷺ used to take a bath from a single vessel.[46]

---

46 Sunan b. Majah – Sahih Hadith

Hadith 47

أَخْبَرَنِي مُحَمَّدُ بْنُ قُدَامَةَ، قَالَ حَدَّثَنَا جَرِيرٌ، عَنْ مَنْصُورٍ، عَنْ زِيَادِ بْنِ عَمْرِو بْنِ هِنْدٍ، عَنْ عِمْرَانَ بْنِ حُذَيْفَةَ، قَالَ كَانَتْ مَيْمُونَةُ تَدَّانُ وَتُكْثِرُ فَقَالَ لَهَا أَهْلُهَا فِي ذَلِكَ وَلَاَمُوهَا وَوَجَدُوا عَلَيْهَا فَقَالَتْ لاَ أَتْرُكُ الدَّيْنَ وَقَدْ سَمِعْتُ خَلِيلِي وَصَفِيِّي صَلَّىٱللَّهُعَلَيْهِوَسَلَّمَ يَقُولُ : « مَا مِنْ أَحَدٍ يَدَّانُ دَيْنًا فَعَلِمَ اللَّهُ أَنَّهُ يُرِيدُ قَضَاءَهُ إِلاَّ أَدَّاهُ اللَّهُ عَنْهُ فِي الدُّنْيَا » .

It was narrated that 'Imran b. Hudayfah, Allah be pleased with him, said: "Maymunah used to take out (interest free) loans frequently, and some of her family criticized her and denounced her for that. She said: 'I will not stop taking loans, for I heard the one who is most beloved to me صَلَّىٱللَّهُعَلَيْهِوَسَلَّمَ, say: "If someone intends to take out a loan, and Allah knows that they intend to pay it back, Allah will pay it back for them in this world."[47]

---

47 Sunan al-Nasa'i – Hasan Hadith

Hadith 48

أَخْبَرَنَا إِبْرَاهِيمُ بْنُ سَعِيدٍ الْجَوْهَرِيُّ، قَالَ حَدَّثَنَا مُحَمَّدُ بْنُ فُضَيْلٍ، عَنِ الْحَسَنِ بْنِ عُبَيْدِ اللَّهِ، عَنْ هُنَيْدَةَ الْخُزَاعِيِّ، عَنْ أُمِّهِ، عَنْ أُمِّ سَلَمَةَ، قَالَتْ كَانَ رَسُولُ اللَّهِ صَلَّى اللَّهُ عَلَيْهِ وَسَلَّمَ يَأْمُرُ بِصِيَامِ ثَلَاثَةِ أَيَّامٍ أَوَّلِ خَمِيسٍ وَالِاثْنَيْنِ وَالِاثْنَيْنِ .

It was narrated that Umm Salamah, Allah be pleased with her, said: "The Messenger of Allah used to order fasting three days: The Monday and Thursday of the first week, and the Monday of the following week."[48]

---

48 Sunan al-Nasa'i – Sahih Hadith

Hadith 49

أَخْبَرَنَا قُتَيْبَةُ، قَالَ حَدَّثَنَا سُفْيَانُ، عَنْ عَمَّارٍ الدُّهْنِيِّ،
عَنْ أَبِي سَلَمَةَ، عَنْ أُمِّ سَلَمَةَ، أَنَّ النَّبِيَّ صَلَّى اللهُ عَلَيْهِ وَسَلَّمَ
قَالَ : «إِنَّ قَوَائِمَ مِنْبَرِي هَذَا رَوَاتِبُ فِي الْجَنَّةِ» .

It was narrated from Umm Salamah, Allah be
pleased with her, that the Prophet ﷺ said:
"The columns of this pulpit of mine will be erected
in paradise."[49]

---

49 Sunan al-Nasa'i – Sahih Hadith

Hadith 50

حَدَّثَنَا الْعَبَّاسُ بْنُ الْوَلِيدِ بْنِ مَزْيَدٍ، قَالَ أَخْبَرَنِي أَبِي

قَالَ، حَدَّثَنَا الأَوْزَاعِيُّ، قَالَ حَدَّثَنَا يَحْيَى بْنُ أَبِي كَثِيرٍ،

عَنْ نَافِعٍ، عَنْ أُمِّ سَلَمَةَ، أَنَّهَا ذَكَرَتْ لِرَسُولِ اللَّهِ

صَلَّى اللَّهُ عَلَيْهِ وَسَلَّمَ ذُيُولَ النِّسَاءِ فَقَالَ رَسُولُ اللَّهِ

صَلَّى اللَّهُ عَلَيْهِ وَسَلَّمَ " يُرْخِينَ شِبْرًا " . قَالَتْ أُمُّ سَلَمَةَ إِذًا

يَنْكَشِفَ عَنْهَا . قَالَ " تُرْخِي ذِرَاعًا لاَ تَزِيدُ عَلَيْهِ "

.

It was narrated from the mother of the believers
Umm Salamah, Allah be pleased with her: She
mentioned women's hems to the Messenger of Allah
صَلَّى اللَّهُ عَلَيْهِ وَسَلَّمَ, and the Messenger of Allah صَلَّى اللَّهُ عَلَيْهِ وَسَلَّمَ
said: "Let it flow downwards a full hand span."
Umm Salamah said: "However, that will uncover
(her feet)!" He صَلَّى اللَّهُ عَلَيْهِ وَسَلَّمَ said: "Then let it flow a

forearm's length, but no more than that."[50]

---

50 Sunan al-Nasa'i – Sahih Hadith

Hadith 51

حَدَّثَنَا وَاصِلُ بْنُ عَبْدِ الأَعْلَى الْكُوفِيُّ، حَدَّثَنَا مُحَمَّدُ بْنُ فُضَيْلٍ، عَنْ عَبْدِ اللهِ بْنِ عَبْدِ الرَّحْمَنِ أَبِي نَصْرٍ، عَنْ مُسَاوِرٍ الْحِمْيَرِيِّ، عَنْ أُمِّهِ، عَنْ أُمِّ سَلَمَةَ، قَالَتْ قَالَ رَسُولُ اللهِ صَلَّى اللَّهُ عَلَيْهِ وَسَلَّمَ : " أَيُّمَا امْرَأَةٍ مَاتَتْ وَزَوْجُهَا عَنْهَا رَاضٍ دَخَلَتِ الْجَنَّةَ " .

Umm Salamah, Allah be pleased with her, narrated the Messenger of Allah ﷺ said: "If a woman dies while her husband is pleased with her, then she enters Paradise."[51]

---

51 Sunan al-Tirmidhi – Hasan Hadith

Hadith 52

حَدَّثَنَا أَبُو بَكْرِ بْنُ أَبِي شَيْبَةَ، حَدَّثَنَا خَالِدُ بْنُ مَخْلَدٍ،
عَنْ مُوسَى بْنِ يَعْقُوبَ، حَدَّثَنِي أَبُو عُبَيْدَةَ بْنُ عَبْدِ
اللهِ بْنِ زَمْعَةَ، عَنْ أَبِيهِ، عَنْ أُمِّ سَلَمَةَ، زَوْجِ النَّبِيِّ ـ
صَلَّى اللهُ عَلَيْهِ وَسَلَّمَ ـ قَالَتْ قَالَ رَسُولُ اللهِ ـ
صَلَّى اللهُ عَلَيْهِ وَسَلَّمَ: «إِذَا شَرِبْتُمُ اللَّبَنَ فَمَضْمِضُوا فَإِنَّ لَهُ
دَسَمًا».

It was narrated that Umm Salamah, the wife of the
Prophet, Allah be pleased with her, said: "The
Messenger of Allah ﷺ said: 'If you drink
milk, then you must rinse out your mouths. That is
because there is some greasiness in it [meaning the
milk]."[52]

---

52 Sunan b. Majah – Hasan Hadith

Hadith 53

وَعَنْ أَمِّ سَلَمَةَ رَضِيَ اَللَّهُ عَنْهَا قَالَتْ: قَالَ رَسُولُ اَللَّهِ
صَلَّى اَللَّهُ عَلَيْهِ وَسَلَّمَ تَقْتُلُ عَمَّارًا اَلْفِئَةُ اَلْبَاغِيَةُ.

Umm Salamah, narrated that the Messenger of Allah
ﷺ said: "The transgressing party will kill
'Ammar ['Ammar b. Yasir, Allah be pleased with
him]."[53]

---

53 Sahih Muslim – Sahih Hadith

Hadith 54

حَدَّثَنَا يَعْقُوبُ بْنُ حُمَيْدِ بْنِ كَاسِبٍ، حَدَّثَنَا عَبْدُ الْعَزِيزِ بْنُ مُحَمَّدٍ الدَّرَاوَرْدِيُّ، عَنْ عُبَيْدِ اللَّهِ بْنِ عُمَرَ، عَنْ إِبْرَاهِيمَ بْنِ مُحَمَّدِ بْنِ عَبْدِ اللَّهِ بْنِ جَحْشٍ، عَنْ أَبِيهِ، عَنْ زَيْنَبَ بِنْتِ جَحْشٍ، أَنَّهُ كَانَ لَهَا مِخْضَبٌ مِنْ صُفْرٍ قَالَتْ فَكُنْتُ أُرَجِّلُ رَأْسَ رَسُولِ اللَّهِ صَلَّى اللهُ عَلَيْهِ وَسَلَّمَ فِيهِ .

It was narrated from (the mother of the believers) Zaynab bint Jahsh, Allah be pleased with her, that she had a tub that was made from brass. She said: "I would comb the hair of the Messenger of Allah in it."[54]

---

54 Sunan b. Majah – Hasan Hadith

Hadith 55

أَخْبَرَنِي أَحْمَدُ بْنُ يَحْيَى الصُّوفِيُّ، قَالَ حَدَّثَنَا أَبُو نُعَيْمٍ،
قَالَ حَدَّثَنَا عِيسَى بْنُ طَهْمَانَ أَبُو بَكْرٍ، سَمِعْتُ
أَنَسَ بْنَ مَالِكٍ، يَقُولُ كَانَتْ زَيْنَبُ بِنْتُ جَحْشٍ
تَفْخَرُ عَلَى نِسَاءِ النَّبِيِّ صَلَّى اللَّهُ عَلَيْهِ وَسَلَّمَ تَقُولُ : إِنَّ اللَّهَ
عَزَّ وَجَلَّ أَنْكَحَنِي مِنَ السَّمَاءِ . وَفِيهَا نَزَلَتْ آيَةُ
الْحِجَابِ .

Anas b. Malik, Allah be pleased with him, said: (The
wife of the Messenger of Allah) Zaynab bint Jahsh,
Allah be pleased with her, used to boast to the other
wives of the Prophet ﷺ and say: "Allah
married me to him from above the Heavens." And
the verse of Hijab was revealed concerning her.[55]

---

55 Sunan al-Nasa'i – Sahih Hadith

Hadith 56

حَدَّثَنَا دَاوُدُ بْنُ أُمَيَّةَ، حَدَّثَنَا سُفْيَانُ بْنُ عُيَيْنَةَ، عَنْ
مُحَمَّدِ بْنِ عَبْدِ الرَّحْمَنِ، مَوْلَى أَبِي طَلْحَةَ عَنْ كُرَيْبٍ،
عَنِ ابْنِ عَبَّاسٍ، قَالَ : خَرَجَ رَسُولُ اللهِ
صَلَّى اللهُ عَلَيْهِ وَسَلَّمَ مِنْ عِنْدِ جُوَيْرِيَةَ - وَكَانَ اسْمُهَا بَرَّةَ
فَحَوَّلَ اسْمَهَا - فَخَرَجَ وَهِيَ فِي مُصَلَّاهَا وَرَجَعَ وَهِيَ
فِي مُصَلَّاهَا فَقَالَ "لَمْ تَزَالِي فِي مُصَلَّاكِ هَذَا" .
قَالَتْ نَعَمْ . قَالَ " قَدْ قُلْتُ بَعْدَكِ أَرْبَعَ كَلِمَاتٍ ثَلَاثَ
مَرَّاتٍ لَوْ وُزِنَتْ بِمَا قُلْتِ لَوَزَنَتْهُنَّ سُبْحَانَ اللهِ
وَبِحَمْدِهِ عَدَدَ خَلْقِهِ وَرِضَا نَفْسِهِ وَزِنَةَ عَرْشِهِ وَمِدَادَ
كَلِمَاتِهِ " .

Abdullah b. Abbas, Allah be pleased with him,
narrated, that the Messenger of Allah صَلَّى اللهُ عَلَيْهِ وَسَلَّمَ
went out from (his wife) Juwayriyyah, Allah be

pleased with her. (It was known that) earlier her name was Barrah, and he (the Messenger of Allah ﷺ) changed it. When he went out she was in her place of worship, and when he returned (back home) she was in her place of worship.

He asked: Have you been in your place of worship all this time? She said: Yes. He then said: Since leaving you [earlier today] I said four phrases three times, which, if weighed against all that you have said [during this period], would still prove to be heavier: And they are "Glory be to Allah", and I begin with His praise, to the number of His creatures, in accordance with His good pleasure, to the weight of His throne, and to the ink [meaning extent] of His words.[56]

---

56 Sunan Abu Dawud – Sahih Hadith

Hadith 57

حَدَّثَنَا أَبُو الْيَمَانِ، أَخْبَرَنَا شُعَيْبٌ، عَنِ الزُّهْرِيِّ، قَالَ
أَخْبَرَنِي سَالِمُ بْنُ عَبْدِ اللَّهِ، أَنَّهُ سَمِعَ عَبْدَ اللَّهِ بْنَ
عُمَرَ ـ رضى الله عنهما ـ يُحَدِّثُ أَنَّ عُمَرَ بْنَ
الْخَطَّابِ حِينَ تَأَيَّمَتْ حَفْصَةُ بِنْتُ عُمَرَ مِنْ خُنَيْسِ
بْنِ حُذَافَةَ السَّهْمِيِّ وَكَانَ مِنْ أَصْحَابِ رَسُولِ اللَّهِ
صَلَّى اللَّهُ عَلَيْهِ وَسَلَّمَ قَدْ شَهِدَ بَدْرًا تُوُفِّيَ بِالْمَدِينَةِ قَالَ عُمَرُ
فَلَقِيتُ عُثْمَانَ بْنَ عَفَّانَ فَعَرَضْتُ عَلَيْهِ حَفْصَةَ
فَقُلْتُ إِنْ شِئْتَ أَنْكَحْتُكَ حَفْصَةَ بِنْتَ عُمَرَ. قَالَ
سَأَنْظُرُ فِي أَمْرِي. فَلَبِثْتُ لَيَالِيَ، فَقَالَ قَدْ بَدَا لِي أَنْ لاَ
أَتَزَوَّجَ يَوْمِي هَذَا. قَالَ عُمَرُ فَلَقِيتُ أَبَا بَكْرٍ فَقُلْتُ
إِنْ شِئْتَ أَنْكَحْتُكَ حَفْصَةَ بِنْتَ عُمَرَ. فَصَمَتَ أَبُو
بَكْرٍ، فَلَمْ يَرْجِعْ إِلَيَّ شَيْئًا، فَكُنْتُ عَلَيْهِ أَوْجَدَ مِنِّي
عَلَى عُثْمَانَ، فَلَبِثْتُ لَيَالِيَ، ثُمَّ خَطَبَهَا رَسُولُ اللَّهِ

صَلَّى اللَّهُ عَلَيْهِ وَسَلَّمَ فَأَنْكَحْتُهَا إِيَّاهُ، فَلَقِيَنِي أَبُو بَكْرٍ
فَقَالَ لَعَلَّكَ وَجَدْتَ عَلَيَّ حِينَ عَرَضْتَ عَلَيَّ حَفْصَةَ
فَلَمْ أَرْجِعْ إِلَيْكَ قُلْتُ نَعَمْ. قَالَ فَإِنَّهُ لَمْ يَمْنَعْنِي أَنْ
أَرْجِعَ إِلَيْكَ فِيمَا عَرَضْتَ إِلاَّ أَنِّي قَدْ عَلِمْتُ أَنَّ رَسُولَ
اللَّهِ صلى الله عليه وسلم قَدْ ذَكَرَهَا، فَلَمْ أَكُنْ
لِأُفْشِيَ سِرَّ رَسُولِ اللَّهِ صَلَّى اللَّهُ عَلَيْهِ وَسَلَّمَ، وَلَوْ تَرَكَهَا
لَقَبِلْتُهَا.

Abdullah b. Umar narrated (that his father) Umar b. al-Khattab, Allah be pleased with them, said, "When (my daughter) Hafsa bint Umar lost her husband Khunays b. Hudhayfah al-Sahmi who was one of the companions of the Messenger of Allah ﷺ and had fought in the battle of Badr and had died in Madinah, I met up with Uthman b. Affan and suggested that he should marry Hafsa saying, "If you wish, I will marry Hafsa the daughter of Umar to you,' on that, he said, 'I will think it over.' I waited for a few days and then he said to me. 'I am of the opinion that I shall not marry at the present time.'

Then I met Abu Bakr and said, 'if you wish, I will marry you, Hafsa the daughter of Umar.' He kept quiet and did not give me any reply and I became angrier with him than I was with Uthman. Some days later, the Messenger of Allah ﷺ asked for her hand in marriage and I married her to him. Later on, Abu Bakr met me and said, "Perhaps you were angry with me when you offered me Hafsa for marriage and I gave no reply to you?' I said, 'Yes!'

Abu Bakr said, 'Nothing prevented me from accepting your offer except that I had prior knowledge that the Messenger of Allah ﷺ had referred to the issue of (marrying) Hafsa, and I did not want to disclose the secret of the Messenger of Allah ﷺ, yet had he declined in marrying her I most certainly have accepted her."[57]

---

57 Sahih al-Bukhari – Sahih Hadith

Hadith 58

أَخْبَرَنَا إِسْمَاعِيلُ بْنُ مَسْعُودٍ، قَالَ حَدَّثَنَا خَالِدٌ، عَنْ

أَشْعَثَ، عَنِ الْحَسَنِ، عَنْ سَعْدِ بْنِ هِشَامٍ، عَنْ عَائِشَةَ،

أَنَّ رَسُولَ اللَّهِ صَلَّى اللَّهُ عَلَيْهِ وَسَلَّمَ نَهَى عَنِ التَّبَتُّلِ .

It was narrated from (the mother of the believers) -
Aisha, Allah be pleased with her, that the Messenger
of Allah ﷺ forbade celibacy.[58]

---

58 Sunan al-Nasa'i – Sahih Hadith

Hadith 59

أَخْبَرَنَا عَلِيُّ بْنُ خَشْرَمٍ، قَالَ أَنْبَأَنَا عِيسَى بْنُ يُونُسَ،
عَنِ ابْنِ أَبِي ذِئْبٍ، عَنِ الْحَارِثِ بْنِ عَبْدِ الرَّحْمَنِ، عَنْ
أَبِي سَلَمَةَ، عَنْ عَائِشَةَ، أَنَّ النَّبِيَّ صَلَّى اللَّهُ عَلَيْهِ وَسَلَّمَ قَالَ :
" فَضْلُ عَائِشَةَ عَلَى النِّسَاءِ كَفَضْلِ الثَّرِيدِ عَلَى سَائِرِ
الطَّعَامِ " .

It was narrated from Aisha, Allah be pleased with
her, that the Prophet said: "The superiority of Aisha
to other women is like the superiority of pieces of
bread in a vegetable or meat broth [Tharid] in
relation to other kinds of food."[59]

---

59 Sunan al-Nasa'i – Hasan Hadith

Hadith 60

أَخْبَرَنَا إِسْحَاقُ بْنُ إِبْرَاهِيمَ بْنِ حَبِيبِ بْنِ الشَّهِيدِ،
قَالَ حَدَّثَنَا يَحْيَى بْنُ يَمَانٍ، عَنْ سُفْيَانَ، عَنْ عَاصِمٍ،
عَنِ الْمُسَيَّبِ بْنِ رَافِعٍ، عَنْ سَوَاءٍ الْخُزَاعِيِّ، عَنْ
عَائِشَةَ، قَالَتْ كَانَ النَّبِيُّ صَلَّى اللهُ عَلَيْهِ وَسَلَّمَ يَصُومُ الاِثْنَيْنِ
وَالْخَمِيسَ .

It was narrated that Aisha, Allah be pleased with her,
said: "The Messenger of Allah ﷺ used to be
most observant in fasting on Mondays and
Thursdays."[60]

---

60 Sunan al-Nasa'i – Hasan Hadith

Hadith 61

حَدَّثَنَا أَبُو بَكْرِ بْنُ أَبِي شَيْبَةَ، وَعَلِيُّ بْنُ مُحَمَّدٍ، وَعَبْدُ
الرَّحْمَنِ بْنُ إِبْرَاهِيمَ، قَالُوا حَدَّثَنَا أَبُو أُسَامَةَ، قَالَ
حَدَّثَنَا هِشَامُ بْنُ عُرْوَةَ، عَنْ أَبِيهِ، عَنْ عَائِشَةَ، قَالَتْ
كَانَ رَسُولُ اللَّهِ ـ ﷺ ـ يُحِبُّ الْحَلْوَاءَ وَالْعَسَلَ .

It was narrated that (the mother of the believers)
Aisha, Allah be pleased with her, said: "The
Messenger of Allah ﷺ loved sweets and
honey."[61]

---

61 Sunan b. Majah – Sahih Hadith

Hadith 62

حَدَّثَنَا أَبُو بَكْرِ بْنُ أَبِي شَيْبَةَ، حَدَّثَنَا خَالِدُ بْنُ مُخَلَّدٍ،
حَدَّثَنِي سَعِيدُ بْنُ مُسْلِمِ بْنِ بَانَكَ، قَالَ سَمِعْتُ عَامِرَ
بْنَ عَبْدِ اللهِ بْنِ الزُّبَيْرِ، يَقُولُ : حَدَّثَنِي عَوْفُ بْنُ
الْحَارِثِ، عَنْ عَائِشَةَ، قَالَتْ قَالَ لِي رَسُولُ اللهِ
صَلَّىٰاللهُعَلَيْهِوَسَلَّمَ : '' يَا عَائِشَةُ إِيَّاكِ وَمُحَقَّرَاتِ الأَعْمَالِ
فَإِنَّ لَهَا مِنَ اللهِ طَالِبًا ''

It was narrated that Aisha, Allah be pleased with her,
said: "The Messenger of Allah ﷺ said to me:
'O Aisha, beware of evil deeds that are regarded as
insignificant, for they have a pursuer from Allah.
(meaning that they have accountability to Allah)."[62]

---

62 Sunan b. Majah – Sahih Hadith

Hadith 63

حَدَّثَنَا أَبُو كُرَيْبٍ، مُحَمَّدُ بْنُ الْعَلاءِ وَإِبْرَاهِيمُ بْنُ
مُوسَى قَالاَ حَدَّثَنَا ابْنُ أَبِي زَائِدَةَ، عَنْ أَبِيهِ، عَنْ خَالِدِ
بْنِ سَلَمَةَ، عَنِ الْبَهِيِّ، عَنْ عُرْوَةَ، عَنْ عَائِشَةَ، قَالَتْ
كَانَ النَّبِيُّ صَلَّى اللَّهُ عَلَيْهِ وَسَلَّمَ يَذْكُرُ اللَّهَ عَلَى كُلِّ أَحْيَانِهِ .

Aisha, Allah be pleased with her, said that the Messenger of Allah صَلَّى اللَّهُ عَلَيْهِ وَسَلَّمَ remembered Allah during all occasions.[63]

---

63 Sunan b. Majah – Sahih Hadith

Here ends the 63 Jewels of
Hadith, and with Allah
is the Success.

Parting gifts for our readers.

Imam Malik's Love for the Ahl al-Bayt

Ja'far, the son of Sulayman, was the Abbasid governor of Madinah.

Ja'far flogged Imam Malik, to the point that he passed out. He was then carried outside in this state and set upon a donkey to be paraded around the city of Madinah.

When Imam Malik awoke and saw himself in this state, he cried out, "I bear witness to you (Ja'far) that I have made my beating a lawful act for you (so you are not punished)!"

Later on, people asked Imam Malik about this and he said, "I was afraid of dying and meeting the Prophet ﷺ with the shameful knowledge that one of his family members could enter the Fire because of what he did to me."

When, al-Mansur was told of what happened he told Imam Malik to take retaliation on Ja'far, but Imam Malik refused, saying to him, "I seek refuge in

Allah! Every time the whip left my body I made it lawful because of his kinship to the Messenger of Allah."

Imam Ja'far's Gift[64]

A man came all the way from Mecca and then fell asleep upon arriving in the city of Madinah. When he awoke, he thought his bag had been stolen.

He saw Imam Ja'far al-Sadiq, and seized him by the collar, saying, "I know you have taken my bag!"

The Imam said, "How much money was in it?"

He, the man, said, "I had a thousand Dinars in it."

Imam Ja'far took him to his own place of residence in Madinah and gave the man a thousand Dinars.

When the man returned home, he saw that his bag was there all along!

This made the man apologetically come back to Imam Ja'far - bringing back the money. However, the Imam did not accept it saying,

---

64 Related in al-Risalah al-Qushayriyyah

"We will not take back what we have given." The man said, "Who is this person?" They said, "He is Imam Ja'far al-Sadiq, Allah is well pleased with him."

Alhamdulillah[65]

It is mentioned that Imam Ja'far al-Sadiq, Allah be well pleased with him, said, "Reciting Alhamdulillah, [Praise be to Allah] is a way of praising Allah with the attributes with which He has described Himself. The word praise [Hamd] in this case is used because it is made up of the three letters Ha, Meem, and Dal.

1) The letter Ha' symbolizes oneness [Wahdaniyya],
2) The letter Meem stands for dominion [Mulk), and
3) The letter Dal symbolizes the reality that Allah goes on forever and ever [Daymumiya].

This is the real meaning of the phrase Alhamdulillah."

---

65 Related in al-Risalah al-Qushayriyyah

LUQMAN AL-ANDALUSI

LUQMAN AL-ANDALUSI

JEWELS OF THE AHL AL-BAYT

LUQMAN AL-ANDALUSI

LUQMAN AL-ANDALUSI

LUQMAN AL-ANDALUSI